D0610190

After Eeyore

Nicola Davies

First performed at
The London Play Festival

Especial thanks to Donna Richards,
the definitive Sister Bernice.

First impression—2000

ISBN 1 85902 948 5

© Nicola Davies

Nicola Davies has asserted her right under the
Copyright, Designs and Patents Act, 1988, to be
identified as Author of this Work.

Application for performance, professional and amateur,
should be made to Nicola Davies at Gomer Press.

Printed in Wales at
Gomer Press, Llandysul, Ceredigion SA44 4QL

Introduction

Despite its comforting title, Nicola Davies's *After Eeyore* does not pay homage to pots of honey, the wide-open spaces of the Hundred Acre Wood nor the lighthearted frolics of Winnie the Pooh. By way of contrast, the play's title underscores the disparity between blithe cheerfulness (seen here in the guise of a school play) and the real life business of maintaining relationships, which can be fraught and painful.

These troubled relationships take place in two rather claustrophobic, closed settings—a convent school and a family living room; the play depicts the emotional journeys of their occupants over a decade. A young vulnerable schoolgirl in need of emotional support and tender care is shown affection and sympathy by her English teacher, a nun, who also directs her in the school play about Winnie the Pooh. The girl and the nun develop strong feelings for one another.

Ten years on, the schoolgirl, now a young widow and teacher herself, returns to her childhood home to recover from the drawn-out death of her husband. Her relationship with her own widowed mother is still troubled and her return revives and deepens her earlier schoolgirl passion for the Sister who is now Mother Superior of the convent.

Through manipulating the time sequence deftly, Nicola Davies indicates how we can carry our personal difficulties across the years. Misunderstandings with those closest to us become entrenched and we can become mired in past behaviours. For most of the play, Esther and her mother are incapable of advancing their relationship beyond Esther's surly dismissal of her mother's rather fussy attempts to help her only child. Similarly, the emotionally limited environment of the convent makes it almost impossible for Sister Bernice and her former pupil to declare their true feelings.

The proscenium arch stage with its missing 'fourth wall' has allowed closed settings to be used to great effect in post-war British drama. Nicola Davies is aware of the dramatic power such a closed setting can have in performance. The emotional intensity of *After Eeyore*, trapped as it is within the four walls of convent school and living room, offers strong roles for actresses. To convey the emotional terrain of the play is equally a challenge for director and set designer.

Beyond the stage, the play might also appeal to older teenagers who might recognise in the central characters of the play their own complex need for emotional support alongside a wilful desire for independence. The text, even without performance, has much to offer.

Anna Marie Taylor
[University of Wales, Swansea]

Characters

Mother Superior .... the former Mother Superior of the convent

Sister Bernice .... A nun; later, the present Mother Superior

Mrs Clay .... Esther's mother

Esther Clay .... (later, Esther Morton)

Father Michael .... a priest

Sister Angela .... a nun

The action of the play takes place in two locations: Mrs Clay's kitchen and a study in the convent. (A divided set has worked very successfully).

The flashback scene in the convent is made apparent to the audience by Esther's appearance as a schoolgirl.

The Prologue is most easily performed in front of a screen, or curtains.

NOTE: An additional scene is included as an appendix and is intended mainly for background information.

Prologue

Mother Superior is sitting at the table. Bernice knocks at the door.

SUPERIOR   Come in.
           (Sister Bernice comes in with an armful of papers.)
BERNICE   Mother. You sent for me. I've brought the accounts.
SUPERIOR   Bernice. How very prompt you are.
BERNICE   You've been up all night again, haven't you?
           (Mother Superior is overcome by a fit of coughing. Bernice dashes for the water jug and pours her a glass of water.)
BERNICE   Sip it. Slowly. Better?
SUPERIOR   Bernice. I coughed.
BERNICE   I can't bear it.
SUPERIOR   Have we really spent this much on scouring powder?
BERNICE   Are you feeling better?
SUPERIOR   Sister. Please. This dying is bad enough without you drawing attention to it every five minutes.
BERNICE   Don't die. Please . . .
SUPERIOR   It comes to us all, Bernice. Now, these accounts . . .
BERNICE   How can you carry on so calmly? So accepting?
SUPERIOR   Accepting? That would be too easy, wouldn't it? I fear Death, Sister. And recoil from the pitiful attempts of this ageing body to carry out its former duties. But I am also the Mother Superior of a convent, child. A nun. I mean to die well.
BERNICE   This will be such a cold place without you.
SUPERIOR   You should not have loved me so much. Perhaps I should have said this before. You're such a warm little creature. You must not allow yourself to be diverted from your path.
BERNICE   My path?
SUPERIOR   Very soon, I will be gone and you will be sitting here.
BERNICE   No! No! I'm still not sure about being a nun, let alone Mother Superior. If it wasn't for the children . . .
SUPERIOR   Ah yes. The children. Tell me, how is the school production coming along?
BERNICE   We're having a little trouble with the costumes. Magdalen's making her usual fuss about the sewing.

SUPERIOR	This will be your last production. Make the most of it.
BERNICE	I can't give up the children. That would be too cruel.
SUPERIOR	I'm sure you will still retain some contact with children. But you must learn to keep them at a distance. They come to us for such a short time, then out into the world, to marry, have families, *(with meaning)* lead their own lives . . . You're good with children. I remember when you first came to us. I found you comforting one of our boarders. A child crying for her Daddy. A small child in the arms of a nun. It made a pretty picture. *(Shakes her head.)* But this is not a picture-book world. Soon, it will be time for us both to move on.
BERNICE	A cold time. I followed the sun here. But I no longer feel its warmth. There is only darkness now and the occasional candle-flame flickering in the night.
SUPERIOR	Do not look to candle flames. One is apt to hold one's breath in case they go out.
BERNICE	Mother?
SUPERIOR	Do not seek the company of other human beings. Accept your destiny. You are meant to walk alone.
BERNICE	No! I can walk out of here if I choose. Other people have done it. Father Aarons left the order to get married last week, didn't he? *He* chose not to walk alone. And what about Sister Davina?
SUPERIOR	Oh, Davina. The vanishing nun.
BERNICE	They found her clothes on the beach last year, didn't they? No sign of a body. Magdalen says she ran off with her guitar teacher.
SUPERIOR	Bernice, your place is here.
BERNICE	No! No!
	(Mother Superior leans towards Bernice, to comfort her, but is overtaken by a fit of coughing. Bernice sees to her.)

END OF PROLOGUE

Act One: Scene One

THE PRESENT: Esther sits at a table, marking a pile of exercise books. We hear Mrs Clay calling.

MRS CLAY   Esther, I'm home
            (*Esther takes no notice. Mrs Clay comes in, carrying shopping bags.*)
MRS CLAY   Esther . . . there you are. You wouldn't believe how busy it is in town. Esther, what are you doing?
ESTHER   What does it look like? Marking English books.
MRS CLAY   Should you be doing that?
ESTHER   (*Deliberately misunderstanding her mother.*) They should have been marked last term. Still, better late than never.
MRS CLAY   I didn't mean that.
ESTHER   I know what you meant, Mother. You want me to 'take it easy'. But I can't just sit here all day, pricking my thumbs.
MRS CLAY   (*helpfully*) Twiddling.
ESTHER   Pardon?
MRS CLAY   It's *twiddling*, not *pricking*. You *twiddle* your thumbs.
ESTHER   (*barely suppressing a smile*) Ah. Yes. Twiddling.
MRS CLAY   (*discomfited*) It is twiddling, I'm sure of it.
ESTHER   Yes, Mother. Of course it's twiddling. (*Smiles.*) 'By the twiddling of my thumbs, something feeble this way comes.'
MRS CLAY   I don't think I'll ever understand you, Esther.
ESTHER   Lucky you.
            (*She puts her pen down, giving up the marking as a lost cause, and walks over to the window, facing the audience. We see a more thoughtful side to her.*)
MRS CLAY   I'll go and unpack the shopping then. I went to the supermarket on the way back from work. This nice man came along to help me with the packing. His name was George. Very efficient he was, too. And so polite. I offered him a tip, but he wouldn't take it. Said he was just doing his job. I said 'George, we could use you in the bakery.' He was so helpful. Pity he's not here now.

(*She picks up her bags, then stands there as if hoping for some response. After a few seconds, Esther turns round.*)

ESTHER   I can't stand this emotional blackmail. If you want help, ask . . . Now, do you want me to help you unpack?

MRS CLAY   Only if you want to.

ESTHER   Of course I don't want to. Why should I want to fill shelves with tins of baked beans and catfood?

MRS CLAY   Catfood? Why catfood? We haven't got a cat.

ESTHER   I know that. Delete *catfood*. Mother, what I'm trying to say is that unpacking shopping gives me no pleasure. But if you want me to help you, I will.

MRS CLAY   No, no. I can manage.
            (*She trots off with her shopping bags. Esther returns to the window.*)

ESTHER   (*to herself*) What a cow you are, Esther Clay.
            (*She looks across the window; the thoughtful look on her face again. Mrs Clay returns.*)

MRS CLAY   Would you like a cup of tea? I brought some cream cakes home from the bakery . . . Esther, come away from the window. The garden's not very cheerful this time of year.

ESTHER   I'd forgotten how near the school is; you can almost see it from here, can't you? (*forcing a laugh*) I thought I saw a nun just now.

MRS CLAY   A nun? In our garden? What was she doing there?

ESTHER   I wish you'd listen. I said I *thought* I saw a nun.

MRS CLAY   Well, I wouldn't put it past them. Sometimes, when I'm drawing the curtains at night, I look out and instead of trees, I see nuns standing there in the twilight. Those women. Your father used to call them the Android Sisters.
            (*Esther returns to her books, then turns to go out of the room.*)

MRS CLAY   Where are you going?

ESTHER   I've left my mark book upstairs.
            (*She goes out. Mrs Clay goes to the kitchen and returns with two mugs of tea and a plate of cream cakes. Esther comes in carrying a small teddy-bear by one leg.*)

MRS CLAY   What's that you've got there?

ESTHER   You should know. It was inside my bed.

MRS CLAY   It's your little old Pookie. I had him dry-cleaned for you.

ESTHER   Why?

MRS CLAY	Why? Well, dear, he needed cleaning.
ESTHER	I mean, why put him in my bed?
MRS CLAY	Comfort. Remember how you used to nurse him in that shawl?
ESTHER	Comfort? *(She looks horrified.)* Are you out of . . . Here, *you* take him. You nurse him. *(She throws him at her mother, who gives him a little pat and sits him on a chair.)*
MRS CLAY	Tea, Esther?
ESTHER	*(She takes the cup)* Why don't you make dear little old Pookie a cup of tea? *(She puts her tea down and goes back to the window.)*
MOTHER	Esther. Your tea's getting cold.
ESTHER	That shrub's grown well, hasn't it? The one Andrew gave you. I remember how worried he was that it wouldn't take. He even phoned you to remind you to mulch it. Funny, isn't it? He's dead and the shrub's flourishing.
MRS CLAY	Oh, Esther. I'm so glad.
ESTHER	*(mischievously)* Glad Andrew's dead?
MRS CLAY	Esther, really! Of course I'm not glad he's dead. What a thing to say. I'm glad to hear you talk about him. It's the first time you've mentioned him since . . .
ESTHER	Since he died?
MRS CLAY	Yes. That. You need to talk about him. It helps.
ESTHER	I see. Who does it help? *(Pause)* I've been wondering if it was a such a good idea to come back here.
MRS CLAY	Not come back? Stay by yourself in that empty flat? I wouldn't have dreamt of leaving you there on your own.
ESTHER	Bad move, mother. I felt safer there.
MRS CLAY	Safer? There?
ESTHER	No ghosts. Just an empty house . . . Empty. You're right . . . This tea is cold.
MRS CLAY	I'll make you another one. Here, give me your cup. *(She hurries out. Esther goes over to the teddy-bear. She buries her face in his fur.)*

End of SCENE

Act One: Scene Two

FLASHBACK: Esther is 18 years old. Father Michael is asleep in the study. Sister Bernice rushes in and scans the room. She is hyperactive, masking tension.

MICHAEL	(*waking suddenly*) Eh? What?
BERNICE	Father. I didn't see you. Did I wake you?
MICHAEL	I was not asleep, Sister.
BERNICE	No, of course not, Father. I, too, think best with my eyes closed. (*She starts her search with the bookcase.*)
MICHAEL	You should knock before entering. That unchannelled energy of yours. Self-control, Sister. Always remember, self-control.
BERNICE	Indeed, Father. (*She moves on, to the cupboards.*)
MICHAEL	What would the Reverend Mother say to see you lacking control, Sister?
BERNICE	She would say that sometimes it is difficult to distinguish between self-control and rigor-mortis. (*She lifts cushions.*) You haven't seen a tail, have you?
MICHAEL	A tail, Sister?
BERNICE	We had it at Dress Rehearsal, Father.
MICHAEL	What would a tail be doing in here? A tail does not walk by itself.
BERNICE	(*smiling*) No, indeed. That's very good, Father. 'A tail does not walk by itself.' Yes, very droll. It's Eeyore's tail, Father. You know . . . Winnie-The-Pooh. The school play.
MICHAEL	Ah. The school play. Has it come round again so soon?
BERNICE	Haven't you noticed all the activity? We've tried to involve the entire school this year. If they're not in the chorus, they're painting woodland scenes on the back-cloth. The sixth formers are playing the large animals and the little ones from the prep school are playing Piglet and Roo. Hence the tail; it's Eeyore's.
MICHAEL	And what part are you playing, Sister?
BERNICE	I'm in the wings, Father.
MICHAEL	(*raising an eyebrow*) An angel, perhaps?

BERNICE   An angel? In Winnie-the-Pooh? No, Father, I'm in the wings, directing operations. And searching for tails.

MICHAEL   Have you tried looking on the stage? It's surely not in here, Sister.

BERNICE   Eeyore left the tail here when she brought me an essay. She had her costume with her. Sister Magdalen hasn't attached the tail yet. She couldn't decide whether to sew it on or attach it with a large nappy-pin. Poor little tail-less donkey.

MICHAEL   Ah, the donkey. An animal in low esteem.

BERNICE   Oh, she'll be alright when we've found her tail.

MICHAEL   A lost tail. I wonder if I can incorporate that idea into one of my Scripture lessons. The donkey cannot perform without her tail. How much worse must it be for those who go about their everyday tasks, but have lost their souls? Children learn so much better from anecdotes. I shall start the lesson with the story of your search for the donkey's tail.

BERNICE   A tail told by an *(whispers)* idiot.

MICHAEL   Bernice?

BERNICE   I was merely quoting Shakespeare, Father.

MICHAEL   Ah, Shakespeare. I have been meaning to talk to you about Shakespeare. Next year, you must perform one of the Bard's plays. Nothing too profound. Not a tragedy. But definitely Shakespeare.

BERNICE   I see. Nothing too profound. Which of his works would you recommend? *A Midsummer Night's Dream*, perhaps? I understand it contains scenes of unrestrained behaviour in a pastoral setting.
            *(The priest looks at her, then laughs despite himself.
            She searches some more.)*

MICHAEL   What would I do without you to hold a mirror before me, Sister? Am I really that pompous?

BERNICE   *(hiding a smile)* Just occasionally, Father. *(She sits down.)* Well, there's nowhere left to look. The tail can't be in here. I was so sure it was.
            (Now she's sitting down, she begins to look worried. Even Michael notices.)

MICHAEL   Something else is troubling you, Sister. What is it ?

BERNICE   Mother Superior. It's strange to see her so ill.

MICHAEL   She's not taken to her bed yet, Sister.

BERNICE   Not everyone dies in bed. Remember Good Queen Bess?

MICHAEL   Before my time . . . Oh, you mean Good Queen Bess.

BERNICE   Yes, Father. She refused to die in bed. I think she stood up for as long as she could, in an effort to fool The Grim Reaper. She must have been so afraid.

MICHAEL   Mother is not afraid . . . of anyone.

BERNICE   No, she's not. But she's not quite ready to die yet. She sent for me today . . . to go over the accounts . . . I can't bear to think of this place without her.

MICHAEL   You will have to, some time.

BERNICE   I have to concentrate on the school play. I've just been calming down the Milligan twins. Caitlin turned over two pages when Pamela was playing Piglet's solo. Pamela said she'd done it on purpose. The older girls are far more trouble than the little ones, Father . . . And now it's the tail. So you see, I'm kept busy. *(She shivers)*

MICHAEL   Are you cold, Sister?

BERNICE   Don't you . . . don't you ever want to leave here for a warmer place?

MICHAEL   Hell, you mean?
             (Bernice smiles, then controls herself as she realises he's serious.)

BERNICE   I meant . . . Father, don't you ever crave human love?

MICHAEL   *(dryly)* Is this a proposal, Sister?
             (Bernice looks at him and bursts out laughing, a little too loudly.)

BERNICE   Take no notice of me, Father. I've got a lot on my mind today. *(Quietly)* First, Mother . . . then . . . I am about to blow out a candle. Oh, Father, it will be so lonely without her.

MICHAEL   You will not be alone, Sister. You will always have my ear.

BERNICE   Thank you, Father. It's a relief to know I shall not lose an ear as well as a tail. Well, I've looked everywhere. You're right, Father. The tail must be elsewhere.
             (We hear a far-off buzzer.)

MICHAEL   Was that the bell? Is that the time? I shall have to be going. *(He stands up and sees the tail.)* Well, well. What do we have here? Your tail has been under me all this time, Sister.

(He hands Bernice the tail and is on his way out. Esther, wearing the donkey head, bounds into the room and into him. Bernice tries not to show her pleasure at seeing Esther.)

ESTHER   Father, I'm sorry. Are you alright?

MICHAEL   Is that you in there, Esther?

ESTHER   Yes, Father. Did I hurt you?

MICHAEL   Luckily, no. Where is your uniform, Esther?

ESTHER   My tie, you mean? It's in my pocket, Father. It didn't go with my head, so I took it off.

MICHAEL   You should have removed your head and left your tie on.

ESTHER   H'm . . . Yes, Father.

MICHAEL   I'll be off then and leave you to your rehearsals.

(They wait until he's shut the door before bursting into laughter.)

BERNICE   Poor man.

ESTHER   When I was in Prep School, I was a little scared of him, you know. I thought he was so clever. We all did. We used to laugh at his jokes, too . . . Is that my tail? Where was it?

BERNICE   Father Michael was sitting on it.

(Esther takes it gingerly, then waves it about, wrinkling her nose. Bernice smiles, then shakes her head . . . 'Now, now Esther.')

BERNICE   So, tell me, why are you still wearing that donkey head?

ESTHER   *(removing the head)* Oh, it makes the little ones laugh. *(she hiccoughs)* It's alright, Sister. I'm not drunk. Winnie's mother sent her a little something to keep her spirits up. We only had a spoonful each.

BERNICE   *(gently teasing)* What size spoon?

ESTHER   Now, now, Sister. You're not to tell me off. I'm so happy.

BERNICE   Are you, little donkey?

ESTHER   Silly isn't it . . . for Eeyore to be happy.

BERNICE   *(pulling herself together, distancing herself from Esther.)* The exams are over. The disastrous dress-rehearsal augurs well for this evening's performance. And you are looking forward to your new life at university, no doubt. Why shouldn't you be happy?

ESTHER   What's bothering you? Is it the Milligans? Don't worry. They're fine now. We gave them some of Winnie's

	medicine and they're playing Chopsticks together. It's because I'm leaving, isn't it? Don't be sad. I'll write to you every week. And I'll be back here at weekends.
BERNICE	I think not. You will forget me once you start your new life.
ESTHER	Forget you? You know I won't forget you.
BERNICE	Oh, there will be memories. But you'll be far too busy to find time for letter-writing and visiting. New friends. Boy-friends.
ESTHER	I don't understand. What are you saying?
BERNICE	I have a present for you, Esther. I was going to give it to you after the performance, but as you are here . . . I'm afraid there was no time to wrap it.
	(*She goes to the cupboard for a book. She gives it to Esther.*)
ESTHER	*Jane Eyre. (turns to the fly-leaf)* 'To a hard-working student, wishing her every success in her new life.' (*flatly*) Thank you. I already have a copy.
BERNICE	Esther. You're not making this easy for me.
ESTHER	Making what easy? Are you trying to say goodbye to me?
BERNICE	I have already said goodbye to you.
ESTHER	When?
BERNICE	In my prayers.
ESTHER	You said goodbye to me and I wasn't even there?
BERNICE	I asked God to look after you for me.
ESTHER	You left me a message with God? Well, he never delivered it. Be your own messenger.
BERNICE	Esther. Please. It seemed the best way.
ESTHER	For you, you mean. The best way for you.
BERNICE	No. For you.
ESTHER	Coward! You coward!
BERNICE	Esther, please. You must learn to control your emotions.
ESTHER	Why? I'm not a nun.
BERNICE	But I am . . . I think it is time you went, Esther. Aren't you supposed to be running through her entrances with the little piglet? Here, take your mask . . . and your book.
	(*Esther picks up the book, then deliberately drops it to the floor.*)
ESTHER	If that's what you want. I'll go this time. But I'll be

back. And then, then you'll be begging me to stay. You will. You'll see.

BERNICE Tonight, after the performance, you will be leaving us. Do not return. I do not wish to see you again. Ever.

ESTHER Oh yes, you do.

(Michael comes in and looks from one to the other.)

MICHAEL Bernice. I heard voices raised. Is anything the matter?

(Esther, tear-stained, grabs the donkey-head and pushes her way past him, slamming the door behind her.)

BERNICE Poor little Esther. She's a little nervous about her stage debut tonight. Highly strung, poor child.

MICHAEL *(sagely)* That will be the examination results, Sister.

BERNICE *(barely able to conceal her impatience)* The what?

MICHAEL Her A-level results. When are they out, Sister?

BERNICE Out? Oh, yes. August.

MICHAEL That will be it then, Sister. The strain of waiting for results, coupled with working towards the performance . . .

(Bernice is now wholly distracted.)

BERNICE I . . . excuse me, Father. *(She runs out.)*

Act One: Scene Three

PRESENT DAY: The living-room. Mrs Clay is at breakfast, reading the newspaper. On the table are toast, jam and marmalade, a jug of coffee etc. Esther, wearing a dressing-gown, comes in yawning.

MRS CLAY You're up early .

ESTHER I couldn't sleep *(she helps herself to coffee.)*

MRS CLAY Esther, here's a coincidence.

ESTHER What is? *(she helps herself to toast and marmalade.)*

MRS CLAY There's a job here for a primary teacher. Summer term. Mornings only.

ESTHER So?

MRS CLAY It would suit you, wouldn't it? Get you back in the swing of things.

ESTHER I am in the swing of things, Mother. In fact, I was thinking of packing my case and swinging back to London tomorrow.

MRS CLAY	But . . .
ESTHER	Funnily enough, I rang my headmistress yesterday and she offered me a job, full time. That supply teacher they got to take my class for the term is off sick. So I can walk back into my old job. It will be good to see Year Four again.
MRS CLAY	But . . .
ESTHER	Don't try to stop me.
MRS CLAY	I wasn't going to. I think you're doing the right thing going back to work. Sitting around the house isn't doing you much good, is it? I just thought you might like this job, being it's in your old school.
ESTHER	My old school?
MRS CLAY	The convent. You could stay here. You wouldn't have to make any meals. Esther, I'd rather you didn't go back. You haven't cried yet.
ESTHER	Cried? Me? What are you on about now?
MRS CLAY	You haven't cried yet. Not at the funeral. Nor since. You have to cry.
ESTHER	Do I? Even if I did, it would be for the wrong reasons.
MRS CLAY	No, not the wrong reasons. I know how everything gets bottled up inside. Talk to me, Esther. Let me help you.
ESTHER	Mother, leave it there.
MRS CLAY	I know what you're going through, Esther.
ESTHER	You mean, one head on the pillow where once there were two. Wearing masks in public and crying after everyone's gone home and left you alone.
MRS CLAY	Oh, Esther. I know . . . I understand.
ESTHER	You ought to . . . I'm pretty much quoting you. You used to tell me all about it from the time I was seven. But I don't feel the way you did when my Da. . . father died. Emptiness. That's all I feel. Empty.
MRS CLAY	That's natural. Your emotions will return in time. You miss Andrew so much, you have to put up barriers, to keep going.
ESTHER	I wish you'd listen! I don't miss him. I do not miss Andrew. If I miss anything at all, it's the patterns. There was a structure to my days. Sitting by the bedside. Dosing him with pain-killers. Little green ones

	in the morning. Multi-coloured capsules at night. He liked the blue ones best. He pretended they were Viagra. In a way, I miss all that. But I don't miss Andrew. I can hardly remember what he looked like. Come to think of it, I can hardly remember anything of our life together. He's been dead ten days and it's as if he never existed.
MRS CLAY	You don't mean that.
ESTHER	Don't I? Than why did I say it?
MRS CLAY	Reaction. False feelings. You think you mean it but you don't, really. You did love Andrew.
ESTHER	(*Wearily*) If you say so, Mother.
MRS CLAY	You're in shock. Give it time. Later, you'll start to remember your life together.
ESTHER	Believe what you like. It doesn't matter.
MRS CLAY	You did love Andrew. I have proof. Concrete proof.
ESTHER	Concrete? You don't mean that inscription you put on his stone, do you? 'Beloved husband of Esther'.
	(*Mrs Clay goes to the sideboard and takes out a small piece of paper.*)
MRS CLAY	If I didn't know better, I'd think you had no heart. Here's your proof.
ESTHER	That piece of paper?
MRS CLAY	(*reads aloud*) 'I will always love you. Always.'
ESTHER	So?
MRS CLAY	I found that in Andrew's wallet. After he died.
ESTHER	Well, well. Good for Andrew. I wouldn't have felt so bad all this time if I knew he had a mistress.
MRS CLAY	Esther, really! You come out with the strangest things. Of course he didn't have a mistress. You wrote that.
ESTHER	Don't be silly.
MRS CLAY	See for yourself. It's in your handwriting.
	(*She hands it over. Esther looks at the note and is taken aback. She recovers herself and is about to tear it up, but her mother intervenes.*)
MRS CLAY	No. Don't do that. You mustn't tear it up.
ESTHER	Why not?
MRS CLAY	One day, you'll want to look at it and be reminded how much you loved Andrew.
ESTHER	Mother, this is nothing to do with Andrew.

MRS CLAY	It isn't?
ESTHER	Look. I don't know what that note was doing in his wallet. Or, come to think of it, what *you* were doing in his wallet. But that note wasn't meant for Andrew.
MRS CLAY	Esther? Who was it meant for, then?
ESTHER	Is that a note of censure in your voice?
MRS CLAY	I'm sorry. I understand. He was so ill. No one could blame you for seeking comfort elsewhere.
ESTHER	That's big of you. But you don't have to try so hard to be understanding. It was nothing like that. I didn't 'seek comfort elsewhere.' Not Esther The Ice-maiden.
MRS CLAY	The Ice-maiden?
ESTHER	Didn't you know? That was what Andrew used to call me 'The Ice-maiden'. Mother, that note was written years ago. I was in the sixth form when I wrote it. I was Eighteen. Eighteen . . . He was Uncle Andrew then, wasn't he? The Andrew who used to to meet me from school or take us to the pictures. I thought you'd given my father the push and stuck Andrew in his place.
MRS CLAY	Esther! But you never said.
ESTHER	I was seven.
MRS CLAY	I wouldn't have survived your father's death without Andrew. I was in such a state. Andrew was so . . .
ESTHER	Helpful. So useful. Such a comfort.
MRS CLAY	Esther?
ESTHER	I remember running into your bedroom one morning, and there he was, Andrew, comforting you in your bed. Yours and my father's.
MRS CLAY	Your father was dead. I loved him but he was gone. I was so lonely. I'm sorry. It never happened again.
ESTHER	Of course not. If you really loved my father, you can't have got much comfort from having another man in your bed. I understand. What I don't understand is how I ended up married to Andrew.
MRS CLAY	I tried to talk you out of it. I said to wait till you got your degree. But there was no stopping you.
ESTHER	Of course. I was going to walk out of University, wasn't I? Fancy my forgetting that. Andrew persuaded me to stay. If it hadn't been for him, there'd have been no degree . . . Maybe I married him out of gratitude.

MRS CLAY	Gratitude? No. You were so determined. You loved him alright.
ESTHER	Not again . . . Mother, that note. In his wallet, you say?
MRS CLAY	Creased, as if he'd read it hundreds of times. He must have thought you meant it for him.
ESTHER	*(Showing emotion for the first time.)* I hope so.
MRS CLAY	But, Esther . . . if it wasn't meant for Andrew . . .
ESTHER	In a way this *is* proof. This note. Not proof of my my love for Andrew, proof that once I felt intensity.
MRS CLAY	I don't believe you didn't love him. Not after the way you nursed him when he was ill.
ESTHER	What option did I have? He was dying.
MRS CLAY	But they said you sat with him all day.
ESTHER	I did. I'd never seen death at close quarters before.
MRS CLAY	Esther!
ESTHER	You wanted me to talk. I'm talking.
MRS CLAY	He said you held his hand for hours.
ESTHER	'He said'. 'They told you'. Have you been spying on me?
MRS CLAY	He used to ring me sometimes. He was so afraid.
ESTHER	Andrew rang you? Why? *(Pause)* Well, it doesn't matter now, does it? Yes, I held his hand and he held on to mine. I think he thought my healthy blood would seep through his skin and bring him back to life.
MRS CLAY	They said you were holding his hand when he died.
ESTHER	'They' were right. I held his hand. He held mine. I was afraid to let go in case his hand came off in mine. I thought I would never be able to free myself, he held on so tightly.
MRS CLAY	Oh, Esther.
ESTHER	There you have it. I sat alone in that dark room, his dead hand in mine, waiting for someone to free me.
MRS CLAY	I didn't know.
ESTHER	And what would you have done if you had?
MRS CLAY	I might have been able to help.
ESTHER	You mean like when you helped my father by shoving him into a hospice? At least *I* stayed with *my* husband.
MOTHER	Esther. I . . . I was too upset . . .
	(Esther looks at her mother . . . better do something before she starts crying.)

ESTHER	I'm sorry. That was uncalled for . . . It was a long time ago. Mother, you're not going to turn the tap on, are you? Crying doesn't solve anything.
MRS CLAY	You're so cold towards me, Esther. What happened to that loving child? That little girl who cried on her first day at school because she didn't want her mother to leave her?
ESTHER	(*Bitterly*) What happened to the mother who cried with her?
MRS CLAY	I should have taken you away from that convent school after your father . . . You took so long to settle. First, you wanted to be a boarder; then, when you were a boarder you wanted to be a day girl.
ESTHER	That's not true. I never wanted to be a boarder.
MRS CLAY	You used to tell me what a good time boarders had.
ESTHER	I was seven. How did I know what it would be like?
MRS CLAY	We packed your case together. You were so excited.
ESTHER	(*with genuine emotion*) He didn't want me to go.
MRS CLAY	Esther?
ESTHER	My father didn't want me to go. You sent me away.
MRS CLAY	Is that what you thought? Esther, your father was ill. It was his idea we sent you as a boarder.
ESTHER	I won't listen to this.
MRS CLAY	He decided it was for the best. He didn't want you to watch us . . . him deteriorating.
ESTHER	My father would not have sent me away. I remember him looking at me as I stood by the door, carrying my case. I wanted to give him a goodbye cuddle, but then you came in. 'Time to go, Esther, Uncle Andrew's waiting in the car. Say *See you soon, Daddy*. Wave goodbye.' And I did.
MRS CLAY	You liked being a boarder.
ESTHER	Not that again. Oh, yes. I was the life and soul of the dorm. The nuns who ran it called me *The Mouse*. Esther Clay, the boarder who thought she was in prison.
MRS CLAY	Really, Esther. You make it sound like a life sentence. It was only for a few weeks. Think what it was like for me, having to go to that dreadful hospice every day.
ESTHER	And when I came home, everything was the same, was it?

SILENCE

MRS CLAY	I was lonely too, you know. I lost him too.
ESTHER	But *you* knew. You knew he was dying. I never said a proper goodbye to him. 'See you soon, Daddy.'

LONG SILENCE

I'm sorry. It was all such a long time ago. I was only seven. Of course you couldn't tell me my Daddy was dying. I'm sorry for bringing all this up after twenty years. I didn't realise that little seven-year old had so much to say. (*She reads the crumpled note again, then looks at her watch.*) It's almost 10.00. Aren't you going to be late for work?

MRS CLAY	(*looks at watch*) I don't have to be in till 10.30 on Tuesdays. They've cut my hours at work. People are buying bread in supermarkets these days.
ESTHER	Look, I'm going upstairs to pack my case. It's probably best for both of us if I go back as soon as possible.
MRS CLAY	You don't have to go.
ESTHER	Oh yes, I do.
MRS CLAY	Well, will you at least wait until I come back from Art?
ESTHER	Art?
MRS CLAY	My Art Class. I go straight from work Tuesdays and Thursdays. I wrote and told you about it.

(*Esther has obviously not read her mother's letter, perhaps none of her letters. She tries to cover up; for the moment, Mrs Clay does not acknowledge this, even to herself; she had not realised that her long letters were never read.*)

ESTHER	Your Art class. Yes, of course.
MRS CLAY	Now you will wait till I come back, won't you? (*Esther nods*) I should be back about four. We could have a bit of tea first and then I'll drop you off at the station. Would you like me to find out train times for you?
ESTHER	No. That's alright. I'll ring the station later.

(*Mrs Clay takes the breakfast things out to the kitchen. Esther looks at the newspaper, then makes a sudden dive for it and copies down the telephone number from the advert. She is reading the headlines when her mother comes in, an overall over her clothes, ready for work.*)

MRS CLAY   You sure you'll be alright on your own? You're very welcome to come with me. No one will mind.

ESTHER   I'll be fine, thanks. I might take a walk later.

MRS CLAY   Why not go for a run ? I'm walking to work today, so you can have the car. Karen picks me up after work Tuesdays and takes us both to Art. She'll bring me home. Well, the keys are here. And you know where the car is? Right then. See you later.

(She goes out.)

END OF ACT ONE

Act Two

PRESENT DAY: Front of curtains. The foyer of the convent, indicated by a chair and a statue, perhaps. Sister Angela storms in.

ANGELA Potatoes! Custard! That woman! "Please ensure there are no lumps in the custard today, Sister." I'll give her lumps. That woman. "Have you remembered to immerse the eggs in boiling water, Sister?" I'll give her and her "immersed . . ." *(She kneels)* Help me, Lord. She makes me so angry. I try to talk to her about you and she insists on talking about her stomach. "Sister, the jacket potatoes . . . please remember to scrub the skins thoroughly." All she ever thinks of is food . . .
(A bell rings. Angela gets up, muttering to herself, and goes out. She returns, followed by Esther.)

ESTHER I phoned several times, but I couldn't get an answer. So as I was in the neighbourhood, I thought I'd pop by. I'd like an application form.

ANGELA If you leave your address, I'll pass it on to our headmistress.

ESTHER Oh, no.

ANGELA Pardon?

ESTHER Well, I was rather hoping to discuss the post first. You see, I may be going back to London next week. There are some questions I need to ask.

ANGELA It's the school holidays. Our headmistress is on Retreat.

ESTHER Is there no one else who could speak to me about it? Perhaps . . . perhaps . . . Sister Bernice?

ANGELA Bernice?

ESTHER She used to teach here. English.

ANGELA Our English teachers are Sister Arthur and Mrs Maitland.

ESTHER Would it be possible to find out what happened to Sister Bernice?

ANGELA Are you sure you have come about the post?

ESTHER Oh, yes. But I would like to see Sister Bernice, too. She taught me. English.

ANGELA	I'll see what can be done. Please wait here
	(*Esther paces up and down, takes out the note and reads it, puts it back in her pocket and paces some more. Angela returns.*)
ANGELA	Apparently, your Sister Bernice is our Mother Superior.
ESTHER	She's here then?
ANGELA	She's probably in her office. Who shall I say it is?
ESTHER	Tell her it's Esther.
ANGELA	Just Esther?
ESTHER	Just Esther. She'll know .
	(*Angela goes out, then returns.*)
ESTHER	Have you found her?
ANGELA	She's rather busy, I'm afraid. She said to apologise for not remembering you.
ESTHER	Not remember? Then . . . she's not coming?
ANGELA	I told her you had come to apply for the teaching vacancy. She will try to spare you a few minutes if you are prepared to wait until she's answered her mail.
ESTHER	I'll wait. Here.
ANGELA	(*dryly*) You may have a long wait. Mother's memory is not what it was. She's probably forgotten all about you by now.
	(*Bernice arrives in time to hear Angela's comment. She recognises Esther, but immediately hides it.*)
ANGELA	(*taken aback*) Mother? So soon? Your letters?
BERNICE	Junk mail. (*turns to Esther*) Are you my visitor? Good. I have a visitor. Now I do not have to tidy my bedroom.
ANGELA	Mother! Really!
BERNICE	Bring us some tea please, Angela. Two cups.
	(*Bernice leads the way into the study. Angela goes off in a huff.*)
BERNICE	Sister Angela is too good for her own good. Now, Mary. Tell me. I understand you are here to discuss the post at the Prep school. It is for one term only. Mrs Maitland has taken leave of absence at short notice.
ESTHER	Is it alright to call you Sister? Do you want me to call you Mother Superior?
BERNICE	Indeed not. I am neither your sister nor your mother. You'd think they'd find something more fitting to call the nun-in-charge of a twenty-first century convent, wouldn't you?
ESTHER	I . . . Sister?

BERNICE	*(looks at watch, pointedly)* I understand you have some questions to ask me. Fire away.
ESTHER	*(thrown)* Questions?
BERNICE	You are interested in our post at the school?
ESTHER	Oh. Oh, yes. . . . Would I be required to give religious instruction?
BERNICE	No, Mary, you would not. That is our responsibility. I'm afraid the ways of a convent school are a little strange to you.
ESTHER	Strange? . . . I was just thinking how good it was to be back in this room with you.
BERNICE	Indeed? I'm afraid you have the advantage, Mary. Do I know you?
ESTHER	I'm Esther. We were on stage together.
BERNICE	On stage? Now where would that be? You appear to have confused me with some other nun. Strangers have difficulty telling us apart. Perhaps you were in the chorus line with some other nun.
	(Esther goes to the cupboard and brings out a book.)
BERNICE	Blow on it.
ESTHER	Sister?
BERNICE	That cupboard. We place in it all the books we have no further use for. It will be very dusty.
ESTHER	There's no dust on this one. The Winnie-the-Pooh scrapbook. Photographs taken at Dress Rehearsal. You must remember. You produced it. Pamela Milligan played the piano.
BERNICE	Ah yes, the Milligan twins.
ESTHER	Caitlin turned the pages. Pamela cried throughout the performance; she was frightened Caitlin would drop the piano lid on her fingers again. Where are they now?
BERNICE	Caitlin's in Kent somewhere, nursing the helpless.
ESTHER	And Pamela?
BERNICE	She has three children now. The eldest is in our Junior school. She often visits us to discuss our shortcomings: surely the little one should be on Reading Book Seven and why do we not award more gold stars to the deserving young daughter?
ESTHER	*(slowly)* Strange how . . . you remember them and not me.
	(Bernice hurries to the door, to look for Angela.)

BERNICE   Ah. Here comes Angela with the tea.
(Angela brings in a tray of tea and biscuits.)

BERNICE   On the table, Sister. Thank you. Now, let us see what goodies you have brought us. Sister, is there nothing in the biscuit tin but ginger snaps?

ANGELA   Mother?

BERNICE   Go and ask Magdalen for some of those milk chocolate fancies. The ones you are always nibbling.

ANGELA   Mother! I do not!

BERNICE   No, of course you do not. Poor Angela. Well, off you go.
(Off goes Angela.)

ESTHER   What a look she threw you.

BERNICE   Tonight, when she talks to God, she will tell him about the crotchety nun who tries her patience so. 'If only that Reverend Mother were not here,' she will say, 'I could be a saint.' *(pouring tea)* Do you take sugar?

ESTHER   You know I don't.

BERNICE   Do I now?
(Angela knocks on the door.)

BERNICE   Come in, Sister.
(Angela comes in with a plate of biscuits.)

BERNICE   Let us see what you have brought us this time. That's better. Six chocolate biscuits. Three for each of us . . . It's alright Sister. I will deny myself prunes supper-time.
(Angela looks at Bernice. Is she serious? Is she making fun? She trots off.)

BERNICE   Help yourself to biscuits, Mary.

ESTHER   Stop it! You know my name's not Mary!

BERNICE   I've taught so many girls . . .

ESTHER   That won't wash. You remember the Milligans. No doubt you remember the name of every girl in the Sixth-form . . . except mine. I wonder why. Why won't you remember me?
(She wanders over to the window and looks out across the audience.)

ESTHER   That tree. Magnolia, isn't it? We read our lines under it. Girls and nuns sitting together on the grass, hearing each other's lines. That was a wonderful summer. A perfect time . . . Frances Bishop was Kanga, wasn't she?

	Who was Rabbit? It was one of the nuns, wasn't it? Sister Magdalen. Yes, Sister Magdalen was Rabbit.
BERNICE	*(droll)* Still is.
	(They look at each other and exchange smiles . . . friendly, but not intimate.)
ESTHER	She wore a carrot round her neck, over her rosary.
BERNICE	Whenever she forgot her lines, she nibbled at that carrot. Lines, indeed! *(mimics, good-naturedly)* 'Yes, Pooh.' 'What do **you** think, Pooh?'
ESTHER	After the dress rehearsal, the sixth-form marinated her carrot in brandy. Her performance was inspired. Reverend Mother congratulated her afterwards and was offered a sip of carrot. *(slowly, remembering the emotions of the past.)* You made me up. Dark grey lines about my mouth and a shiny black nose. You encased my hands in black hooves, checked my zip was fastened to the top and wished me luck. When I came on stage, shaking my large donkey ears, your eyes shone approval. Oh, Sister, it all seems so real. It's as if I never left here.
BERNICE	*(trying to recover herself)* I think we have had enough of Winnie-the-Pooh.
ESTHER	Surely not. We've not looked at the photographs yet. I thought I'd forgotten all this. But it's so real. It's like I've gone back ten years. Like the past was just waiting for me to come back. *(opens book)* See. Here I am, in my donkey head. And there you are, patting me on the shoulder.
BERNICE	Close it! Close it, Esther Clay. You may have gone back in time, Esther. But I am very much in the present.
ESTHER	After the dress rehearsal, you gave everyone a flower, but me. You gave me a poem. I learnt it by heart . . . *(recites)* 'The Donkey . . . by G. K.Chesterton . . . Fools, for I also had my hour . . . One far fierce hour and sweet. There was a shout about my ears and palms before my feet.'
BERNICE	And that was your finest hour, was it? Playing Eeyore in Winnie the Pooh?
ESTHER	I did not intend playing Eeyore. I auditioned for Tigger.
BERNICE	Is that why you came back, to complain about the casting? *(PAUSE)* It's always pleasant when former pupils come to visit us. But now, I have other work to attend to.

ESTHER	I came to apply for the post. Had you forgotten?
BERNICE	You forgot that yourself, long ago.
ESTHER	I convinced myself I was just coming here for an application form. But then I realised how much I wanted see you. When you came into the room, everything flooded back. All the feelings I had then. I feel as if I'm eighteen again. As if all that's happened since I left here has been a dream. If I close my eyes, I'm back in my school uniform.
BERNICE	Then open your eyes , Esther.
	(When Esther does so, she looks in wonderment at Bernice, as if she's realising something for the first time.)
ESTHER	After all this time. I can't believe it . . . I feel. *(she struggles for the words)* I feel 'known.' As if, at last, I am known. I feel so alive in your presence. I always did. You really did love me, didn't you?
BERNICE	*(interrupting)* Loved you? Esther, you misunderstand. I felt affection for every girl who passed through my hands.
ESTHER	That's not true. You know it's not. We used to sit for hours together, you and I. Lunch-times. After school.
BERNICE	And what did we talk about, *(mocking)* 'you and I?' What intimate details passed between us?
ESTHER	What?
BERNICE	You have conveniently forgotten the reason we spent so much time together. Your mother demanded it. She wanted you to have every chance of getting your grades.
ESTHER	And what did *you* want?
BERNICE	You were not my best pupil. But you worked hard. I was prepared to devote extra time to helping you. Esther, there was a loneliness in you. It spoke to something in me. I tried to be kind to you because of that. That was all.
ESTHER	Why are you trying to destroy my memories ?
BERNICE	Memories alter with time.
ESTHER	Not mine.
BERNICE	I see. So nothing has happened to you since then. Have you done nothing but relive the several hours we spent together studying Shakespeare?
ESTHER	You told me never to come back.
BERNICE	If I did, it does not seem to have had the desired effect.

ESTHER Why did you send me away?
BERNICE I sent you away? When?
ESTHER You know *when*. So *why?*
BERNICE Esther, if I sent you away, then I must have had good reason . . . No doubt it was to set you on your future path.
ESTHER (*dismissively*) My future?
BERNICE Have you been walking backwards all this time?
ESTHER Not walking, running. Aimlessly . . . breathlessly . . . On all fours. On my little black hooves. Running away from you. (*She stops, hearing herself speak her thoughts aloud for the first time*) . . . and back towards you.
  (*Angela walks in, surprised that Esther is still here.*)
ANGELA I . . . More tea, Mother?
BERNICE We shall make a waitress of you yet, Angela.
ANGELA Mother?
BERNICE If you are a nun, then please go about your many duties, Angela. On the other hand, if you wish us to train you as a waitress, then I will do what I can to obtain a suitable uniform for you. Something a shade less sombre, perhaps, with a hint of knee-cap.
ANGELA Mother?
BERNICE Yes, Angela?
  (*Angela looks at her, is about to speak, then says nothing. She goes out.*)
ESTHER I remember the first time you said *my* name. My first day in the sixth-form. You took the register. When you came to my name, you stopped. You looked at me. You knew me, didn't you? Although it was the first time, it seemed as if you had spoken to me long before.
BERNICE I remember a child sobbing alone in the dormitory.
ESTHER Was that you?
BERNICE I was lonely too. I had begun to wonder if I had done wrong to commit myself to God. I heard you sobbing, and it was as if you were giving voice to my own pain and bewilderment.
ESTHER You held me in your arms while I cried. I felt so safe. So loved. Afterwards, I thought it had been a dream, manufactured out of my own loneliness. No wonder I felt as if I had loved you all my life.

	(*She takes the note and hands it to Bernice. Bernice reads and is taken aback.*)
BERNICE	Esther?
	(*She leans forward. Then looks hard at Esther.*)
BERNICE	I thought . . . *(collects herself)* Come, little donkey, the time has come to tell me the real reason you are here . . . When is the baby due?
ESTHER	How do you know? I didn't tell . . .
BERNICE	I saw it in your eyes just now.
ESTHER	In my eyes? Sister, there's a future in pregnancy testing for you. You could make yourself a fortune. Oh, Sister I'm so lost. Could we not pretend I'm that little girl again? Will you hold me in your . . . .
BERNICE	Don't look back, Esther.
ESTHER	Don't look back? I am back. I'm trapped in time.
BERNICE	You trap yourself. Blame yourself, not Time.
	(*Angela comes in and stares at them pointedly.*)
BERNICE	Angela?
ANGELA	I'm sorry, Mother. I did not realise your visitor was still here.
BERNICE	I was just telling Esther about Time.
ANGELA	Time? Yes. Of course . . . The Reverend Mother is a very busy woman. There are so many calls on her time.
BERNICE	Not *the* time, Angela. I was talking about the *idea* of time. Concepts.
ANGELA	Concepts? You want to discuss concepts?
BERNICE	Esther thinks of Time as a photographer, taking snapshots for an album. The changeless past.
ESTHER	And don't you have any snapshots, any memories?
ANGELA	A nun puts aside personal memories when she enters a convent.
BERNICE	Thank you, Angela. Yes, indeed. Angela has jettisoned all memories of former boyfriends.
ANGELA	Mother!
BERNICE	Oh, dear. Poor Angela. Had you no boyfriends?
ANGELA	Really, Mother!
BERNICE	Did you have no one to love you and to love? Did you give up nothing when you gave yourself to God? . . . I had a boyfriend. So many plans. My wedding-dress all

	cut out and ready to sew. God's voice seemed stronger. I came here.
ESTHER	It's like a harem, isn't it? All these brides of God.
BERNICE	A harem for the more mature lady.
ANGELA	Mother, you mustn't talk like this.
BERNICE	I forgot. Angela would prefer to talk about culinary matters. She makes such lovely sponge-cakes. You must ask her for the recipe when you leave.
	(*Esther laughs. Angela throws her a look.*)
BERNICE	Esther is one of my former pupils. She means you no harm.
ANGELA	And you, Mother?
BERNICE	Well, well. So there is something behind that mask of yours.
BERNICE	Have no fear, Angela. No harm shall come to you. Not while you are clutching that tray. (*Angela goes out.*)
ESTHER	That was cruel . . . .
BERNICE	Just as I bring out the worst in Angela, she has the same effect on me. I thought if she worked under Magdalen in the kitchen, she would learn to be more human. But she has merely learned how to make puddings. Angela thinks Time is grown in the garden.
ESTHER	How do you see Time?
BERNICE	I see Time as a tall clock-tower. One face keeps Greenwich mean-time. Stand before it and you're in step with civilisation. Events line up in order. Yesterday's always the regulation distance behind tomorrow . . . Move to another face of the tower and you discover biological time . . . skin crumples, babies grow, organs succumb to guarantee. All in order. So it seems. Until you move past the face that has no memory, with hands that spin when disaster threatens. At every face of the tower, your time-scale alters. At all but one . . . a golden face, bathed in a clear blue light. The hands seem to have stopped. Only if you stand there for a hundred years, will you see the hands move. God's clock. Do not raise your eyes above it, or the light will burn them.
ESTHER	So that's how you did it.
BERNICE	Esther?
ESTHER	I've always remembered you as an inspired teacher.

	But I wasn't sure how you did it. That was wonderful. If I was eighteen again, I'd follow you anywhere. I thought you were the moon and the sun. So sure, so together.
BERNICE	After the performance, when you were not at the after-show festivities, I went to look for you. The house seemed empty, in darkness, but I knew where you were. As I walked the unlit corridors, I could hear the sound of your voice. At the door I stopped. You were sobbing, like a frightened child. I stood there and turned away.
ESTHER	So you *were* there. I knew it.
BERNICE	I turned away because I could offer you no comfort. I sat in the bright lights of the party , tapping my feet in time to the music. 'Have you seen Esther?' they asked. I shook my head. I had not seen Esther, but I had heard you. And even though you were sobbing, I envied you your tears.
ESTHER	If only I'd known. I packed my case, phoned Mum to come and get me and waited by the gates. That was the last time I was here . . . until now.
BERNICE	This child of yours . . . does it have a father?
ESTHER	What do you mean?
BERNICE	I may have been calling you Mary this long time, but I do not think yours was an immaculate conception. Do you know who the father is?
ESTHER	You thought I was perturbed because I do not know the father? Not know the father? Shame on you *(takes deep breath)* His name is Christopher. We live on a small farm. Sheep blunder into the garden, leaving neat piles of maggot-like droppings. Once, a wild donkey wandered into my garden. In my urban innocence, I went to stroke it. It bared its teeth and tried to bite me. Its tail, caked with manure, swung out at me.
BERNICE	*(coldly)* Do you wish me to appraise your story for style or content?
ESTHER	Y'what?
BERNICE	Winnie the Pooh in the Wasteland. Is that really what happened to Eeyore out in the big world?
ESTHER	You're so protected in here. Why didn't you let *me* become a nun? You prepared me for nothing. For a world that does not exist. Love, Death. They're just concepts to you, aren't they? Just . . .

BERNICE	Esther, don't be afraid. Go back to the father. Marry him.
ESTHER	What are you on about now?
BERNICE	That's what's troubling you, isn't it? Whether to marry the father. Yes, you must marry him.
ESTHER	You don't know what you're saying.
BERNICE	Don't you love him?
ESTHER	I never loved him. I loved someone else, who turned me away. I forgot how to love.
BERNICE	Esther, you mustn't say that.
ESTHER	Why not? It's the truth.
BERNICE	*(straw-clutching)* You must marry the father. For the baby's sake.
ESTHER	*(mocking)* But Sister, I *did* marry the father.
BERNICE	Then there is still hope. You will learn to love him.
ESTHER	That would be difficult *(pause)*. He's dead.
BERNICE	*(taken aback)* Dead? Esther, I'm so sorry. When?
ESTHER	Ten days ago.
BERNICE	Ten days . . . Oh, Esther. I am sorry. So sorry. You must miss him so. Was it a good marriage?
ESTHER	Civilised. Andrew was much older than me. We did the Times crossword together and went to the theatre. He drove me to work and picked me up from work. If I wanted anything, I had only to ask. We never quarrelled.
BERNICE	It sounds like a good marriage, Esther.
ESTHER	Does it? Since he died, I have been examining our marriage. I can't remember why I married him. I used to think that perhaps I'd married him out of jealousy. He was my mother's lover, you see.
BERNICE	Esther. No!
ESTHER	Messy business, the real world, isn't it? You don't know the half of it. I wouldn't let him near me. We had separate bedrooms. Then he became ill. His first operation was successful. I mean, they said he'd be alright. He was so grateful he wasn't going to die. 'Things will be different now,' he said. But then, when they said inoperable, he couldn't take it. He said his life was over and he'd never been happy. He was crying. Begging. I couldn't refuse his last request, could I? He wanted—as if it mattered—he wanted a son to carry on his name. He kept saying, 'Thank you, Esther, forgive me.' Over and over again.

	(She's too upset to realise the effect she's having on Bernice. The nun is sitting in a chair, rocking, her hands clasped in anguish, not prayer.)
ESTHER	I watched him die and . . . I wanted to feel something, anything. I wanted to be capable of love, compassion . . . hate, even. And then he was dead and it meant nothing. *(Pause)* Look what you have done to me.
BERNICE	Esther. Please . . . .
ESTHER	Andrew asked for mercy, too. 'Please God, stop the pain. Give me the chance to do things better. I'll be good . . .' You . . . you wouldn't believe in your God if you'd watched that man die! I prayed for someone to put him out of his pain . . . After he died, I began to see that I was dead too. Only I'd died a long time ago. How does it feel to ruin someone's life?
	(Bernice can't take any more. She starts to sob. Esther looks at her, baffled.)
ESTHER	Please don't cry. Please.
	(Bernice is sobbing now. Heart-rending sobs.)
BERNICE	Forgive me. I did not know. Esther. Not know.
	(Esther gives one cry, then runs over to Bernice and puts her arms round her.)
ESTHER	I'm sorry. I didn't mean to hurt you. I didn't understand. All those things I said just now. I didn't know I was going to say all that. I just wanted to hurt someone . . . you.
	(She wipes Bernice's tears) You mustn't take any notice. Please don't cry. It's not your fault.
BERNICE	I caused you so much pain. I sent you away.
ESTHER	What else could you have done?
BERNICE	But not like that. I was so frightened. I could not let you go. I sent you away on a long lead.
ESTHER	*You* were frightened of *me*?
BERNICE	Not of you. Of myself. Of loving the little Esther too much.
	(She embraces Esther. At the same time, Angela arrives and stands in the doorway. A smile of triumph clouds her face. She's found Bernice out at last, she thinks. She steps forward.)

END OF ACT TWO

Act Three: Scene One

As Bernice and Esther move apart, Bernice sees Angela.

BERNICE	(*trying to act normally*) Angela. I did not see you there.
ANGELA	That's obvious.
BERNICE	Have you been standing there long?
ANGELA	Long enough.
BERNICE	I see.
ANGELA	(*unable to hold back any longer*) Is that all you have to say?
BERNICE	What would you have me say, Angela?
ANGELA	You've plenty to say when you're making fun of me. You . . . you hypocrite! All those fine words about not forming attachments to other nuns. And look at you! You and her!
	(*Bernice is lost for words, vulnerable. Angela, sensing she has struck home, carries on with renewed vigour.*)
ANGELA	Mother Superior! You ought to be ashamed of yourself. I looked up to you! I looked up to you. I put up with all your nonsense because I admired you. You! You . . . make me sick. Kissing her! Holding her! Who do you think you are?
	(*Esther steps forward, to the rescue.*)
ESTHER	I think you'd better stop now, before you make a fool of yourself.
ANGELA	I'm not the fool, madame.
ESTHER	I'm pregnant.
	(*Angela looks at Bernice as if wondering if she is responsible. She becomes confused.*)
ANGELA	Pregnant?
ESTHER	I came for advice. My husband has recently died. I had no one else to turn to.
ANGELA	(*still trying to catch her out*) You came for . . . for the post.
ESTHER	That was one of the options I had to consider, yes. Bereavement. A child on the way. Who else would I turn to for spiritual comfort?

	(Angela looks from one to the other, realising she's made a fool of herself.)
ANGELA	I . . . I . . . I don't know what came over me.
BERNICE	Don't you, Angela?
ANGELA	I . . . Forgive me, Mother.
BERNICE	You must thank the Good Lord, Angela, for allowing you to experience a new emotion, SHAME. It will ensure that you will never again be quite so self-satisfied.
ANGELA	*(flustered)* May I go now, Mother?
BERNICE	Mrs . . . *(turns to Esther)*
ESTHER	Morton.
BERNICE	Mrs Morton will be off soon, Angela. After which, I will be greatly in need of a strong cup of coffee. Would you mind?
ANGELA	No. Yes. Of course not. Mother.
	(She goes out backwards, flustered, red-faced.)
BERNICE	*(quietly)* Thank you.
ESTHER	*(fiercely)* How dare she talk to you like that!
BERNICE	*(laughing gently)* Only you are allowed to talk to me like that, are you?
ESTHER	*(laughs)* I was rather rude to you, wasn't I?
BERNICE	The fruit of familiarity, perhaps?
ESTHER	You've seen me at my worst . . . but you see me at my best, too.
BERNICE	And now you've seen me . . . I've tried so hard to hide my feelings. Angela probably thinks I have none: a sort of android nun.
ESTHER	An android! I think that's how my mother sees you . . . and me. Both of us. It's how I saw myself until now. I seem to have been deceiving myself all these years. I thought I was no longer able to cry. The last time I cried was . . . that night. I think I've been too frightened to cry, in case . . .
BERNICE	In case you would cry for ever.
ESTHER	If only I'd been able to talk to you about Andrew, instead of bottling everything up inside. I could always talk to you, couldn't I? It was like having a wise older sister. And then, the sex thing. I really muddied things up, didn't I? I felt so muddled.
BERNICE	And now? How do you feel now?

ESTHER	I feel . . . well, sort of free. Yes, free. Clear. Well, clearer. I can think more clearly. Yes. Definitely. (*Bernice looks at her askance. they burst out laughing.*) And what about you? Will you be alright?
BERNICE	Me? Oh yes. I shall just have to work a little harder at being an android.
ESTHER	Bernice? I couldn't bear that for you.
BERNICE	Esther, didn't you hear what I said about Time? I meant it. In twenty, perhaps thirty years, I shall be gone from here. No one but you will know my story. I shall be just another nun gone to dust . . . Dear me . . . I'll be quoting Shakespeare next, won't I? Esther, I've no illusions about what will happen here when I die. The Mother Superior who takes my place may well be an Angela-clone who will destroy my work and produce a convent of simpering self-satisfied nuns That is the way of things. (*looks at note*) Still, I have something to remind me of warmer times, don't I?
ESTHER	(*looks at watch*) I ought to be getting back home now.
BERNICE	That would be best. Just in case Angela's on the prowl. Though I think it most unlikely.
ESTHER	I'll come back. Soon.
BERNICE	(*knowing she won't*) Of course.
ESTHER	If I decide to keep . . . I'll bring the baby to see you.
BERNICE	Of course. I shall wheel the pram up and down the grounds and Angela will change the nappies for you. (*They look at each other, then hug once more.*)
ESTHER	Wave to me.
BERNICE	I shall stand by the window and watch you go. (*Esther leaves. Bernice goes to the window. She reads the note.*) (*reads aloud*) I will always love you. Always. (*she waves at Esther, then lowers her arms slowly. She folds the note up, then whispers to herself.*) 'Do not look to candle flames. One is apt to hold one's breath in case they go out.' (*She takes a deep breath*) Goodbye, little donkey. (*She stands there for a few seconds, near to tears. She crosses to the mirror and adjusts her headdress, tucking away stray wisps of hair. She is once again the Mother Superior. There is a knock on the door.*)

BERNICE	Come in.
	(A very contrite Angela comes in with the coffee.)
BERNICE	Angela. How good of you to remember.
ANGELA	Mother, I have something to say.
BERNICE	No need, Angela.
ANGELA	But Mother. I wish to explain.
BERNICE	I know you do, Angela. There is no need.
ANGELA	But Mother. I want you to know . . .
BERNICE	Beating one's breast is best left to the anonymity of the confessional. *(She sips her coffee, then puts the cup down.)* Now, perhaps you would like to accompany me on a walk in the grounds?
ANGELA	A walk? But it's raining.
	(Bernice raises an eyebrow.)
ANGELA	I shall fetch an umbrella on the way out, Mother.
BERNICE	And what shall we discuss as we walk through the shrubbery? Perhaps you would like to look at the small shoots and saplings and discuss parallels with the way Our Lord nurtures the human soul?
ANGELA	Oh yes, Mother. The human soul.
BERNICE	Or shall we discuss the deeper meaning of a biblical text?
ANGELA	As you see fit, Mother.
BERNICE	Then in that case, we shall discuss . . . puddings.
ANGELA	Puddings, Mother?
BERNICE	Yes, puddings. I have been hankering for a chocolate pudding all this week. Have you ever made a chocolate pudding, Angela?
ANGELA	Choc . . . No, Mother.
BERNICE	During our walk, I shall give you several recipes. Egg-white, Angela. We shall begin with egg-white . . .
	(She puts the cup down and steers Angela towards the door.)
BERNICE	The first task is deciding how best to separate the yolk from the albumen.
ANGELA	*(despite herself, a small protest)* Oh, Mother.
	(They go out.)

Act Three: Scene Two

Mrs Clay's living-room. It is empty. Mrs Clay comes in carrying a folder of artwork. She looks around, calls for Esther and goes out. We hear her calling upstairs. Esther comes in. She notices the artwork and begins to look through it. Her mother comes in from the kitchen with a mug of tea.

MRS CLAY	Esther. You're back.
ESTHER	These are good. No, really. I hadn't realised. You're good.
MRS CLAY	I wish you hadn't. I don't like people to look at my . . .
ESTHER	I'm not people. (*She puts the work away.*) Still, if you don't want me to.
MRS CLAY	They're not original. Most of them are copied from postcards.
ESTHER	This is our garden. That's not from a postcard.
MRS CLAY	No. A photograph.
ESTHER	Ah. And the town centre? Another photograph?
MRS CLAY	That's just a pencil sketch.
ESTHER	But it's original?
MRS CLAY	What there is of it.
ESTHER	Well, it's really good. Those shadows. It's very well-observed.
MRS CLAY	You really think so, Esther?
ESTHER	I know so. You don't need to copy from postcards. You ought to concentrate on pencil sketches.
MRS CLAY	Well, I do enjoy that, but . . . you have to try different mediums, even if you don't like working in oils. Miss Hopkirk says we have to experience everything.
ESTHER	No you don't.
MRS CLAY	Esther?
ESTHER	You should stick at what you're good at. I'd like one of your pencil sketches to hang on my walls at home. Framed.
MRS CLAY	You would? Really?
ESTHER	Really. You're very good.
MRS CLAY	Well, thank you, Esther. I'll get onto it tomorrow, first thing.
ESTHER	I'll pay for it.
MRS CLAY	You'll do no such thing.

ESTHER	Oh, yes. You must charge me. Then you can tell that Miss Hopkirk you've made a sale. And when you've done a few more of those sketches, say twenty or thirty of them, I'll organise a little exhibition for you.
MRS CLAY	Would you, Esther?
ESTHER	I mean it. I'm proud of you.
MRS CLAY	That's . . . very kind of you, Esther. Twenty, you say? My own exhibition?
ESTHER	Nothing grand. A room in the local library, perhaps.
MRS CLAY	Perhaps we could include a few paintings by other people. You should see Karen's watercolours. And there's Frank with his still lives. Miss Hopkirk's always asking him who the woman with the enormous breasts is.
ESTHER	Mother, don't get carried away. I'm for you. Miss Hopkirk can exhibit the work done in class. I want a room full of my mother's work. I'm very proud of you, you know.
MRS CLAY	You are?
ESTHER	Of course I am.
MRS CLAY	And I'm very . . .
ESTHER	(*interrupting*) Now don't let's get carried away, Mother.
MRS CLAY	Esther . . . where are my manners? I haven't offered you tea.
ESTHER	No reason you should. I'll make myself a cup in a minute or two. You sit down and enjoy your tea.
MRS CLAY	Esther . . . something's happened to you, hasn't it? You're a lot chirpier.
ESTHER	Chirpier? . . . Yes, perhaps I am.
MRS CLAY	You've been out, haven't you?
ESTHER	I took the car. I hope that's alright?
MRS CLAY	Was there enough petrol in it?
ESTHER	Enough to get me to the garage.
	(*Mrs Clay goes to her handbag and offers Esther money.*)
ESTHER	What's that for?
MRS CLAY	The petrol.
ESTHER	Don't be silly. I only put in a few pounds' worth. And there's plenty left.
MRS CLAY	You went into town then? Did some shopping to cheer yourself up?
ESTHER	I went visiting, actually. An old friend.

MRS CLAY	Wherever you've been, it's done you a lot of good. It doesn't need an expert to see what's happened.
ESTHER	Mother?
MRS CLAY	I don't blame you Esther. Not at all. Other people might say it's too soon. But other people don't realise how empty life can be . . .
ESTHER	(*her first sign of impatience*) Mother! What are you on about now?
MRS CLAY	You can't bring anyone back to life, however much you love them. Andrew wouldn't want you to be unhappy. He'd understand.
ESTHER	Mother, who have you been talking to? You sound like one of those 'counsellors'. I haven't been 'seeking comfort elsewhere'. Well, not in the way you think. I've been visiting an old school friend.
MRS CLAY	That's nice dear. Talking about old times. . . . Did you tell her, Esther?
ESTHER	About Andrew? Oh, yes. And other things. (*quietly*) She'll be so lonely now.
MRS CLAY	Esther?
ESTHER	(*deep breath*) I'm pregnant.
MRS CLAY	Since this morning? (*She realises how silly she is being.*) Oh, dear. What a stupid thing to say.
ESTHER	You don't have to do that. Why do you do it? You're not daft. Why do you say these things?
MRS CLAY	Habit, Esther. And men . . . .
ESTHER	Don't say it.
MRS CLAY	What?
ESTHER	Don't say 'men like it.' Any man who's so insecure he needs a woman to play 'spot the moron' isn't worth bothering over. Stop the games, Mother. It's so wearing. And I need to discuss something with you.
MRS CLAY	It's Andrew's baby, isn't it? Yes, of course it is. Are you pleased?
ESTHER	I think so.
MRS CLAY	Are you keeping it?
ESTHER	I think so.
MRS CLAY	Whatever you decide, I want to be part of it. (*Mrs Clay reaches out to Esther, then changes her mind. Esther ignores the gesture.*)

ESTHER	May I look at the rest of these paintings?
MRS CLAY	Paintings? I can't be bothered with paintings now.
ESTHER	How about a cup of tea, then?
MRS CLAY	No. Don't fob me off, Esther. Please. I want to help.
ESTHER	I know you do. But . . . give me time, Mother. Please.
	(She reaches out and squeezes her mother's shoulder. Mrs Clay pats Esther's hand, then stands back.)
MRS CLAY	Tea, Esther?

THE END

Appendix: Additional Scene

THE PAST: (Sister Bernice is in her early twenties.)
Front of curtains. The Mother Superior is sitting at a table, looking through the convent accounts. Bernice knocks the door.

MOTHER	*(calls)* Come in . . . Ah, Bernice.
BERNICE	You sent for me, Reverend Mother?
MOTHER	Sit down, Bernice. Good. I have sent for you because I understand you have something to say to me.
BERNICE	No, Mother. I don't know why you should think that.
MOTHER	Come Bernice. We have no secrets here.
BERNICE	No, Mother.
MOTHER	How very amenable you are, my dear. One would think you the best of all possible nuns.
BERNICE	*(meekly)* Thank you, Mother.
MOTHER	Please wipe that inane expression from your face . . . Bernice, I understand you are thinking of leaving us.
BERNICE	How could you possible know that? I told no one.
MOTHER	You did not need to. Have you not been wearing obedience like a badge these last weeks? You perform your duties without complaint. Sister Martha thinks you a reformed character. But we know differently, don't we? We have become less important to you, haven't we, now that you are contemplating leaving us?
BERNICE	Yes, I am thinking of leaving.
MOTHER	And how soon would that be, Sister?
BERNICE	Mother?
MOTHER	Did you expect me to plead with you to stay? That would be difficult, knowing how many of your sisters would breathe a sigh of relief to see you go.
BERNICE	Why? I have done nothing to them.
MOTHER	You do not whistle while working, like little Sister Francis. Nor do you praise God for your burdens, as does Sister Jacinta. No, indeed. You have perfected the art of glowering . . . Sister, why did you come to us?
BERNICE	I was so sure. I saw the light so clearly when I was out there in the world. It brought me here . . . and then it abandoned me. Why?

MOTHER	What are you saying, child?
BERNICE	Nothing, Mother. It was a dream, that's all. Now I am awake in an alien place. I mark books, teach the first-formers how to use a dictionary and do the ironing. Day after day.
MOTHER	The light, Bernice. Tell me about that light.
BERNICE	I cannot, Mother. I can't remember what it was like. This place is squeezing the life out of me. I will die if I stay here.
MOTHER	(*dryly*) Indeed you will, Sister. But I do not think it will be possible for you to leave us. It appears you were brought here by God. If you leave us, he will bring you back here again.
BERNICE	No. Don't say that. How can you say that to me?
MOTHER	Bernice. Until today, I saw you as others see you. But now . . . now . . . when you were speaking, I sensed the presence of God. More real than I had ever thought possible.
BERNICE	NO! That was nothing to do with me.
MOTHER	You felt it too, then.
BERNICE	I felt nothing. Nothing. There is no one here but you and me.
MOTHER	I am sure this is where you are meant to be.
BERNICE	I can walk out of here now . . . whenever . . .
MOTHER	Of course you can . . . Bernice, I see now that your breathless spirit heralds a wind of change. You are needed here. I need you.
BERNICE	I can leave here any time I wish . . . I . . . Oh, Mother.
MOTHER	I will watch you with great interest from now on.
BERNICE	Why? Are you making a study of mutiny in a convent?
MOTHER	Good . . . humour oils the wheels, Sister. It will keep that proud spirit of yours in check.
BERNICE	Like my hair, mother.
MOTHER	Your hair?
BERNICE	I used to wear it loose, to my waist. Now it is hidden under this. Mother, I didn't realise how vain I was. Why did God give me such lovely hair if he wanted me to keep it hidden?
MOTHER	My child, at the end of your life, when your hair is but

	a gossamer cap, you will thank God for removing all the trappings of vanity.
BERNICE	Never!
MOTHER	Bernice, you may not think so now . . . .
BERNICE	When I first came here, I did not expect to find myself weighed down by trivia. Mother, I sometimes think that if I could wear my own clothes and display my hair, I could be happy here. Aren't you ashamed of me?
MOTHER	Prawn cocktails, Sister . . . . That is my little weakness. Starter, main course. I dream of throwing up on a surfeit of prawns. So you see, little sister, I cannot censure you for your vanity . . . Well, Bernice, the ironing is piling up, for want of you.
BERNICE	Oh, Mother. I do not want my days to be measured out in scorch-marks. Am I to come to you to share my joy at freeing a saucepan from the blemish of burnt potato or a sheet from extinction? Will years pass so quickly that the steam-iron seems never to leave my hand?
MOTHER	The years will pass, Bernice, but they will not find you the same. The years will pass.